50 Ice Cream and Sorbet Recipes for Home

By: Kelly Johnson

Table of Contents

Ice Cream Recipes:

- Vanilla Bean Ice Cream
- Chocolate Fudge Ice Cream
- Strawberry Ice Cream
- Mint Chocolate Chip Ice Cream
- Cookies and Cream Ice Cream
- Coffee Ice Cream
- Rocky Road Ice Cream
- Pistachio Ice Cream
- Butter Pecan Ice Cream
- Coconut Ice Cream
- Peanut Butter Cup Ice Cream
- Cherry Garcia Ice Cream
- Neapolitan Ice Cream
- Mango Ice Cream
- Raspberry Swirl Ice Cream
- Blueberry Cheesecake Ice Cream
- Caramel Swirl Ice Cream
- Banana Nut Ice Cream
- Lemon Sorbet Ice Cream
- Orange Creamsicle Ice Cream
- Almond Joy Ice Cream
- Chocolate Chip Cookie Dough Ice Cream
- Key Lime Pie Ice Cream
- Red Velvet Ice Cream
- Tiramisu Ice Cream

Sorbet Recipes:

- Lemon Sorbet
- Raspberry Sorbet
- Mango Sorbet
- Strawberry Sorbet
- Orange Sorbet

- Pineapple Sorbet
- Watermelon Sorbet
- Kiwi Sorbet
- Blueberry Sorbet
- Peach Sorbet
- Blackberry Sorbet
- Green Apple Sorbet
- Grape Sorbet
- Coconut Sorbet
- Passion Fruit Sorbet
- Lychee Sorbet
- Pear Sorbet
- Cranberry Sorbet
- Pomegranate Sorbet
- Guava Sorbet
- Plum Sorbet
- Cantaloupe Sorbet
- Fig Sorbet
- Papaya Sorbet
- Honeydew Sorbet

Ice Cream Recipes:

Vanilla Bean Ice Cream

Ingredients:

- 2 cups heavy cream
- 1 cup whole milk
- 3/4 cup granulated sugar
- Pinch of salt
- 1 vanilla bean pod (or 2 teaspoons of vanilla extract)
- 6 large egg yolks

Instructions:

In a medium saucepan, combine the heavy cream, whole milk, sugar, and salt. If using a vanilla bean pod, split it open lengthwise with a knife and scrape out the seeds. Add both the seeds and the pod to the saucepan. If using vanilla extract, skip this step for now.
Heat the mixture over medium heat, stirring occasionally, until it begins to steam. Do not let it boil.
In a separate bowl, whisk the egg yolks until smooth.
Once the cream mixture is steaming, gradually pour about 1/2 cup of the hot mixture into the bowl with the egg yolks, whisking constantly. This tempers the eggs, preventing them from curdling.
Pour the egg mixture back into the saucepan with the remaining cream mixture, stirring constantly.
Cook the mixture over medium heat, stirring constantly, until it thickens slightly and coats the back of a spoon. This usually takes about 5-7 minutes. Do not let it boil.
Once thickened, remove the saucepan from the heat. If you used a vanilla bean pod, remove it from the mixture.
If you didn't use a vanilla bean pod, stir in the vanilla extract at this point.
Pour the mixture through a fine-mesh sieve into a clean bowl to remove any cooked egg bits or vanilla pod remnants. Let it cool to room temperature, then cover and refrigerate for at least 4 hours, or overnight, until thoroughly chilled.
Once chilled, churn the mixture in an ice cream maker according to the manufacturer's instructions until it reaches a soft-serve consistency.
Transfer the churned ice cream to a freezer-safe container and freeze for at least 4 hours, or until firm.
Serve and enjoy your homemade Vanilla Bean Ice Cream!

This recipe makes about 1 quart of ice cream. Feel free to adjust the sweetness or vanilla flavor to suit your taste preferences.

Chocolate Fudge Ice Cream

Ingredients:

- 2 cups heavy cream
- 1 cup whole milk
- 3/4 cup granulated sugar
- Pinch of salt
- 1/2 cup unsweetened cocoa powder
- 4 ounces semisweet chocolate, chopped
- 4 large egg yolks
- 1 teaspoon vanilla extract
- 1/2 cup hot fudge sauce (homemade or store-bought)

Instructions:

In a medium saucepan, combine the heavy cream, whole milk, sugar, cocoa powder, and salt. Whisk until the cocoa powder is fully incorporated.
Heat the mixture over medium heat, stirring occasionally, until it begins to steam. Do not let it boil.
Once steaming, add the chopped semisweet chocolate to the saucepan and stir until completely melted and smooth. Remove from heat.
In a separate bowl, whisk the egg yolks until smooth.
Gradually pour about 1/2 cup of the hot chocolate mixture into the bowl with the egg yolks, whisking constantly. This tempers the eggs, preventing them from curdling.
Pour the egg mixture back into the saucepan with the remaining chocolate mixture, stirring constantly.
Cook the mixture over medium heat, stirring constantly, until it thickens slightly and coats the back of a spoon. This usually takes about 5-7 minutes. Do not let it boil.
Once thickened, remove the saucepan from the heat and stir in the vanilla extract. Transfer the mixture to a clean bowl and cover with plastic wrap, pressing the plastic wrap directly onto the surface of the mixture to prevent a skin from forming. Refrigerate for at least 4 hours, or overnight, until thoroughly chilled.
Once chilled, churn the mixture in an ice cream maker according to the manufacturer's instructions until it reaches a soft-serve consistency.

Once churned, layer the churned ice cream into a freezer-safe container, alternating with spoonfuls of hot fudge sauce. Swirl the fudge sauce into the ice cream using a knife or spatula.

Freeze the ice cream for at least 4 hours, or until firm.

Serve and enjoy your homemade Chocolate Fudge Ice Cream!

Feel free to customize this recipe by adding chopped nuts or extra fudge sauce for a more decadent treat.

Strawberry Ice Cream

Ingredients:

- 1 pound (about 4 cups) fresh strawberries, washed, hulled, and sliced
- 1 cup granulated sugar, divided
- 1 teaspoon lemon juice
- 2 cups heavy cream
- 1 cup whole milk
- 1 teaspoon vanilla extract
- Pinch of salt

Instructions:

In a bowl, combine the sliced strawberries with 1/2 cup of granulated sugar and lemon juice. Stir well to coat the strawberries, then cover the bowl and let it sit at room temperature for about 1 hour. This will allow the strawberries to release their juices and become macerated.

After an hour, transfer the macerated strawberries to a blender or food processor and puree until smooth. You can also leave some chunks for texture if desired.

In a separate mixing bowl, whisk together the heavy cream, whole milk, remaining 1/2 cup of granulated sugar, vanilla extract, and a pinch of salt until the sugar is dissolved.

Add the strawberry puree to the cream mixture and stir until well combined. Transfer the mixture to the refrigerator and chill for at least 2 hours, or until thoroughly chilled.

Once chilled, pour the mixture into an ice cream maker and churn according to the manufacturer's instructions until it reaches a soft-serve consistency.

Transfer the churned ice cream to a freezer-safe container, cover with a lid or plastic wrap, and freeze for at least 4 hours, or until firm.

Serve and enjoy your homemade Strawberry Ice Cream!

This recipe yields about 1.5 quarts of ice cream. For an extra burst of strawberry flavor, you can fold in some diced strawberries during the last few minutes of churning. Enjoy your creamy and fruity treat!

Mint Chocolate Chip Ice Cream

Ingredients:

- 2 cups heavy cream
- 1 cup whole milk
- 3/4 cup granulated sugar
- Pinch of salt
- 1 teaspoon pure peppermint extract
- Green food coloring (optional)
- 1 cup semi-sweet chocolate chips or chunks

Instructions:

In a medium saucepan, combine the heavy cream, whole milk, granulated sugar, and salt. Heat the mixture over medium heat, stirring occasionally, until it begins to steam. Do not let it boil.
Once steaming, remove the saucepan from the heat and stir in the peppermint extract. If desired, add a few drops of green food coloring to achieve the desired mint color. Stir until well combined.
Transfer the mixture to a heatproof bowl and cover with plastic wrap, pressing the plastic wrap directly onto the surface of the mixture to prevent a skin from forming. Chill in the refrigerator for at least 4 hours, or overnight, until thoroughly chilled.
Once chilled, pour the mixture into an ice cream maker and churn according to the manufacturer's instructions until it reaches a soft-serve consistency.
During the last few minutes of churning, add the chocolate chips or chunks and continue churning until evenly distributed.
Transfer the churned ice cream to a freezer-safe container, cover with a lid or plastic wrap, and freeze for at least 4 hours, or until firm.
Serve and enjoy your homemade Mint Chocolate Chip Ice Cream!

Feel free to adjust the amount of peppermint extract to suit your taste preferences. You can also vary the amount of chocolate chips for more or less chocolate in each bite.

Enjoy the refreshing mint flavor combined with rich chocolate pieces in this classic ice cream flavor!

Cookies and Cream Ice Cream

Ingredients:

- 2 cups heavy cream
- 1 cup whole milk
- 3/4 cup granulated sugar
- Pinch of salt
- 1 teaspoon vanilla extract
- 15-20 chocolate sandwich cookies (like Oreos), crushed into small pieces

Instructions:

In a medium saucepan, combine the heavy cream, whole milk, granulated sugar, and salt. Heat the mixture over medium heat, stirring occasionally, until it begins to steam. Do not let it boil.
Once steaming, remove the saucepan from the heat and stir in the vanilla extract. Stir until well combined.
Transfer the mixture to a heatproof bowl and cover with plastic wrap, pressing the plastic wrap directly onto the surface of the mixture to prevent a skin from forming. Chill in the refrigerator for at least 4 hours, or overnight, until thoroughly chilled.
Once chilled, pour the mixture into an ice cream maker and churn according to the manufacturer's instructions until it reaches a soft-serve consistency.
During the last few minutes of churning, add the crushed chocolate sandwich cookies and continue churning until evenly distributed.
Transfer the churned ice cream to a freezer-safe container, cover with a lid or plastic wrap, and freeze for at least 4 hours, or until firm.
Serve and enjoy your homemade Cookies and Cream Ice Cream!

This recipe yields a creamy vanilla ice cream base with delicious chocolate cookie chunks mixed throughout. Feel free to adjust the amount of cookies to suit your preference for more or less cookie pieces in each bite. Enjoy this classic flavor combination that's perfect for any occasion!

Coffee Ice Cream

Ingredients:

- 2 cups heavy cream
- 1 cup whole milk
- 3/4 cup granulated sugar
- Pinch of salt
- 1/3 cup ground coffee beans (medium to coarse grind)
- 5 large egg yolks
- 2 teaspoons pure vanilla extract

Instructions:

In a medium saucepan, combine the heavy cream, whole milk, granulated sugar, salt, and ground coffee beans. Heat the mixture over medium heat, stirring occasionally, until it begins to steam. Do not let it boil.

Once steaming, remove the saucepan from the heat and let the mixture steep for about 20-30 minutes to infuse the coffee flavor. Stir occasionally.

After steeping, strain the mixture through a fine-mesh sieve or cheesecloth into a clean saucepan to remove the coffee grounds. Press down on the grounds to extract as much flavor as possible. Discard the grounds.

In a separate bowl, whisk the egg yolks until smooth.

Gradually pour about 1/2 cup of the warm coffee-infused cream mixture into the bowl with the egg yolks, whisking constantly. This tempers the eggs, preventing them from curdling.

Pour the egg mixture back into the saucepan with the remaining coffee-infused cream mixture, stirring constantly.

Cook the mixture over medium heat, stirring constantly, until it thickens slightly and coats the back of a spoon. This usually takes about 5-7 minutes. Do not let it boil.

Once thickened, remove the saucepan from the heat and stir in the vanilla extract.

Transfer the mixture to a clean bowl and cover with plastic wrap, pressing the plastic wrap directly onto the surface of the mixture to prevent a skin from forming. Chill in the refrigerator for at least 4 hours, or overnight, until thoroughly chilled.

Once chilled, pour the mixture into an ice cream maker and churn according to the manufacturer's instructions until it reaches a soft-serve consistency.

Transfer the churned ice cream to a freezer-safe container, cover with a lid or plastic wrap, and freeze for at least 4 hours, or until firm.
Serve and enjoy your homemade Coffee Ice Cream!

This recipe yields a rich and creamy coffee-flavored ice cream with a delightful caffeine kick. Feel free to adjust the amount of ground coffee beans to suit your preference for a stronger or milder coffee flavor. Enjoy this delicious treat as a dessert or a pick-me-up!

Rocky Road Ice Cream

Ingredients:

- 2 cups heavy cream
- 1 cup whole milk
- 3/4 cup granulated sugar
- Pinch of salt
- 1/2 cup unsweetened cocoa powder
- 1 teaspoon vanilla extract
- 1/2 cup mini marshmallows
- 1/2 cup chopped nuts (such as almonds or walnuts)
- 1/2 cup chopped dark chocolate or semisweet chocolate chips

Instructions:

In a medium saucepan, combine the heavy cream, whole milk, granulated sugar, cocoa powder, and salt. Heat the mixture over medium heat, stirring occasionally, until it begins to steam. Do not let it boil.

Once steaming, remove the saucepan from the heat and stir in the vanilla extract. Stir until well combined.

Transfer the mixture to a heatproof bowl and cover with plastic wrap, pressing the plastic wrap directly onto the surface of the mixture to prevent a skin from forming. Chill in the refrigerator for at least 4 hours, or overnight, until thoroughly chilled.

Once chilled, pour the mixture into an ice cream maker and churn according to the manufacturer's instructions until it reaches a soft-serve consistency.

During the last few minutes of churning, add the mini marshmallows, chopped nuts, and chopped chocolate to the ice cream maker. Continue churning until evenly distributed.

Transfer the churned ice cream to a freezer-safe container, cover with a lid or plastic wrap, and freeze for at least 4 hours, or until firm.

Serve and enjoy your homemade Rocky Road Ice Cream!

This recipe yields a rich chocolate ice cream base with swirls of marshmallows, nuts, and chocolate throughout. Feel free to adjust the amount of marshmallows, nuts, and chocolate to suit your preference for a more or less chunky texture. Enjoy this classic flavor combination that's perfect for any ice cream lover!

Pistachio Ice Cream

Ingredients:

- 2 cups heavy cream
- 1 cup whole milk
- 3/4 cup granulated sugar
- Pinch of salt
- 1 teaspoon pure vanilla extract
- 1 teaspoon almond extract
- 1 cup shelled pistachios, unsalted
- Green food coloring (optional)

Instructions:

In a blender or food processor, pulse the pistachios until finely chopped. Be careful not to over-process; you want some texture remaining.

In a medium saucepan, combine the heavy cream, whole milk, granulated sugar, and salt. Heat the mixture over medium heat, stirring occasionally, until it begins to steam. Do not let it boil.

Once steaming, remove the saucepan from the heat and stir in the vanilla extract and almond extract. Stir until well combined.

Transfer the mixture to a heatproof bowl and cover with plastic wrap, pressing the plastic wrap directly onto the surface of the mixture to prevent a skin from forming. Chill in the refrigerator for at least 4 hours, or overnight, until thoroughly chilled.

Once chilled, strain the mixture through a fine-mesh sieve into a clean bowl to remove any lumps.

Stir in the chopped pistachios and green food coloring (if using) until evenly distributed.

Pour the mixture into an ice cream maker and churn according to the manufacturer's instructions until it reaches a soft-serve consistency.

Transfer the churned ice cream to a freezer-safe container, cover with a lid or plastic wrap, and freeze for at least 4 hours, or until firm.

Serve and enjoy your homemade Pistachio Ice Cream!

This recipe yields a creamy pistachio-flavored ice cream with a lovely green hue and crunchy bits of chopped pistachios throughout. Adjust the amount of green food coloring to achieve your desired shade of green. Enjoy this delightful treat on its own or paired with your favorite desserts!

Butter Pecan Ice Cream

Ingredients:

- 2 cups heavy cream
- 1 cup whole milk
- 3/4 cup granulated sugar
- Pinch of salt
- 4 tablespoons unsalted butter
- 1 cup pecans, chopped
- 1 teaspoon pure vanilla extract

Instructions:

In a medium saucepan, combine the heavy cream, whole milk, granulated sugar, and salt. Heat the mixture over medium heat, stirring occasionally, until it begins to steam. Do not let it boil.
While the cream mixture is heating, melt the butter in a separate skillet over medium heat. Add the chopped pecans and toast them in the butter until fragrant and lightly browned, stirring frequently. This should take about 3-5 minutes. Be careful not to burn the pecans.
Once the cream mixture is steaming, remove the saucepan from the heat and stir in the vanilla extract.
Transfer the mixture to a heatproof bowl and cover with plastic wrap, pressing the plastic wrap directly onto the surface of the mixture to prevent a skin from forming. Chill in the refrigerator for at least 4 hours, or overnight, until thoroughly chilled.
Once chilled, strain the mixture through a fine-mesh sieve into a clean bowl to remove any lumps.
Stir in the toasted pecans and any remaining butter from the skillet until evenly distributed.
Pour the mixture into an ice cream maker and churn according to the manufacturer's instructions until it reaches a soft-serve consistency.
Transfer the churned ice cream to a freezer-safe container, cover with a lid or plastic wrap, and freeze for at least 4 hours, or until firm.
Serve and enjoy your homemade Butter Pecan Ice Cream!

This recipe yields a creamy, nutty ice cream with crunchy toasted pecans and a hint of buttery richness. It's perfect for any occasion and sure to be a crowd-pleaser!

Coconut Ice Cream

Ingredients:

- 2 cans (13.5 oz each) full-fat coconut milk
- 1 cup sweetened shredded coconut
- 3/4 cup granulated sugar
- Pinch of salt
- 1 teaspoon pure vanilla extract

Instructions:

In a saucepan, combine the coconut milk, sweetened shredded coconut, granulated sugar, and salt. Heat the mixture over medium heat, stirring occasionally, until it begins to steam. Do not let it boil.
Once steaming, remove the saucepan from the heat and stir in the vanilla extract. Transfer the mixture to a heatproof bowl and cover with plastic wrap, pressing the plastic wrap directly onto the surface of the mixture to prevent a skin from forming. Chill in the refrigerator for at least 4 hours, or overnight, until thoroughly chilled.
Once chilled, strain the mixture through a fine-mesh sieve into a clean bowl to remove the shredded coconut. Discard the coconut solids.
Pour the strained mixture into an ice cream maker and churn according to the manufacturer's instructions until it reaches a soft-serve consistency.
Transfer the churned ice cream to a freezer-safe container, cover with a lid or plastic wrap, and freeze for at least 4 hours, or until firm.
Serve and enjoy your homemade Coconut Ice Cream!

This recipe yields a creamy and refreshing coconut-flavored ice cream with bits of sweetened shredded coconut throughout. It's perfect for coconut lovers and a delightful treat on a hot day. Feel free to garnish with additional toasted coconut or fresh fruit before serving, if desired. Enjoy!

Peanut Butter Cup Ice Cream

Ingredients:

- 2 cups heavy cream
- 1 cup whole milk
- 3/4 cup granulated sugar
- Pinch of salt
- 1 teaspoon pure vanilla extract
- 1/2 cup creamy peanut butter
- 1 cup chopped peanut butter cups (about 8-10 regular-sized peanut butter cups)

Instructions:

In a medium saucepan, combine the heavy cream, whole milk, granulated sugar, and salt. Heat the mixture over medium heat, stirring occasionally, until it begins to steam. Do not let it boil.
Once steaming, remove the saucepan from the heat and stir in the vanilla extract.
In a separate microwave-safe bowl, microwave the peanut butter for about 30-45 seconds, or until it's softened and slightly runny.
Gradually whisk the softened peanut butter into the hot cream mixture until fully incorporated.
Transfer the mixture to a heatproof bowl and cover with plastic wrap, pressing the plastic wrap directly onto the surface of the mixture to prevent a skin from forming. Chill in the refrigerator for at least 4 hours, or overnight, until thoroughly chilled.
Once chilled, pour the mixture into an ice cream maker and churn according to the manufacturer's instructions until it reaches a soft-serve consistency.
During the last few minutes of churning, add the chopped peanut butter cups to the ice cream maker and continue churning until evenly distributed.
Transfer the churned ice cream to a freezer-safe container, cover with a lid or plastic wrap, and freeze for at least 4 hours, or until firm.
Serve and enjoy your homemade Peanut Butter Cup Ice Cream!

This recipe yields a creamy peanut butter-flavored ice cream with chunks of chocolatey peanut butter cups mixed throughout. It's a decadent treat that's sure to satisfy any peanut butter lover's cravings!

Cherry Garcia Ice Cream

Ingredients:

- 2 cups heavy cream
- 1 cup whole milk
- 3/4 cup granulated sugar
- Pinch of salt
- 1 teaspoon pure vanilla extract
- 1 cup fresh cherries, pitted and chopped
- 1/2 cup dark chocolate chips or chunks

Instructions:

In a medium saucepan, combine the heavy cream, whole milk, granulated sugar, and salt. Heat the mixture over medium heat, stirring occasionally, until it begins to steam. Do not let it boil.
Once steaming, remove the saucepan from the heat and stir in the vanilla extract. Transfer the mixture to a heatproof bowl and cover with plastic wrap, pressing the plastic wrap directly onto the surface of the mixture to prevent a skin from forming. Chill in the refrigerator for at least 4 hours, or overnight, until thoroughly chilled.
Once chilled, pour the mixture into an ice cream maker and churn according to the manufacturer's instructions until it reaches a soft-serve consistency.
During the last few minutes of churning, add the chopped cherries and dark chocolate chips to the ice cream maker and continue churning until evenly distributed.
Transfer the churned ice cream to a freezer-safe container, cover with a lid or plastic wrap, and freeze for at least 4 hours, or until firm.
Serve and enjoy your homemade Cherry Garcia Ice Cream!

This recipe yields a creamy vanilla ice cream base with swirls of fresh cherries and chunks of dark chocolate throughout, reminiscent of the popular store-bought flavor. It's a delightful combination of sweet and tart flavors that's perfect for summer or anytime you're craving a refreshing treat!

Neapolitan Ice Cream

Ingredients:

For Vanilla Ice Cream:

- 2 cups heavy cream
- 1 cup whole milk
- 3/4 cup granulated sugar
- Pinch of salt
- 1 teaspoon pure vanilla extract

For Chocolate Ice Cream:

- 2 cups heavy cream
- 1 cup whole milk
- 3/4 cup granulated sugar
- Pinch of salt
- 1/2 cup unsweetened cocoa powder
- 1 teaspoon pure vanilla extract

For Strawberry Ice Cream:

- 2 cups heavy cream
- 1 cup whole milk
- 3/4 cup granulated sugar
- Pinch of salt
- 1 cup fresh strawberries, hulled and chopped
- 1 teaspoon lemon juice
- 1/2 teaspoon pure vanilla extract

Instructions:

For each flavor, in a medium saucepan, combine the heavy cream, whole milk, granulated sugar, and salt. Heat the mixture over medium heat, stirring occasionally, until it begins to steam. Do not let it boil.
Once steaming, remove the saucepan from the heat and stir in the respective flavorings: vanilla extract for the vanilla ice cream, cocoa powder and vanilla

extract for the chocolate ice cream, and chopped strawberries, lemon juice, and vanilla extract for the strawberry ice cream. Stir until well combined.

Transfer each flavored mixture to a separate heatproof bowl and cover with plastic wrap, pressing the plastic wrap directly onto the surface of the mixture to prevent a skin from forming. Chill each bowl in the refrigerator for at least 4 hours, or overnight, until thoroughly chilled.

Once chilled, pour each flavored mixture into separate sections of an ice cream maker and churn according to the manufacturer's instructions until each flavor reaches a soft-serve consistency.

Once churned, layer each flavor into a freezer-safe container, alternating between vanilla, chocolate, and strawberry layers. You can use a spoon or spatula to spread each layer evenly.

Once all flavors are layered, cover the container with a lid or plastic wrap and freeze for at least 4 hours, or until firm.

Serve and enjoy your homemade Neapolitan Ice Cream!

This recipe yields a classic Neapolitan Ice Cream with layers of creamy vanilla, rich chocolate, and refreshing strawberry flavors. It's perfect for enjoying on its own or as part of an ice cream sundae.

Mango Ice Cream

Ingredients:

- 2 cups ripe mango pulp (fresh or canned)
- 1 cup heavy cream
- 1 cup whole milk
- 3/4 cup granulated sugar
- Pinch of salt
- 1 teaspoon pure vanilla extract

Instructions:

If using fresh mangoes, peel and dice the mangoes. Then, puree the mango flesh in a blender or food processor until smooth. If using canned mango pulp, simply measure out 2 cups.

In a medium saucepan, combine the mango pulp, heavy cream, whole milk, granulated sugar, and salt. Heat the mixture over medium heat, stirring occasionally, until it begins to steam. Do not let it boil.

Once steaming, remove the saucepan from the heat and stir in the vanilla extract. Stir until well combined.

Transfer the mixture to a heatproof bowl and cover with plastic wrap, pressing the plastic wrap directly onto the surface of the mixture to prevent a skin from forming. Chill in the refrigerator for at least 4 hours, or overnight, until thoroughly chilled.

Once chilled, pour the mixture into an ice cream maker and churn according to the manufacturer's instructions until it reaches a soft-serve consistency.

Transfer the churned ice cream to a freezer-safe container, cover with a lid or plastic wrap, and freeze for at least 4 hours, or until firm.

Serve and enjoy your homemade Mango Ice Cream!

This recipe yields a creamy and refreshing mango-flavored ice cream with the sweet and tropical taste of ripe mangoes. It's perfect for enjoying on a hot day or as a refreshing dessert after a meal. Feel free to garnish with fresh mango slices or shredded coconut before serving, if desired. Enjoy!

Raspberry Swirl Ice Cream

Ingredients:

For the Raspberry Swirl:

- 2 cups fresh raspberries (or thawed frozen raspberries)
- 1/4 cup granulated sugar
- 1 tablespoon lemon juice

For the Ice Cream Base:

- 2 cups heavy cream
- 1 cup whole milk
- 3/4 cup granulated sugar
- Pinch of salt
- 1 teaspoon pure vanilla extract

Instructions:

In a saucepan, combine the raspberries, sugar, and lemon juice. Cook over medium heat, stirring occasionally, until the raspberries break down and release their juices, and the mixture thickens slightly, about 5-7 minutes. Remove from heat and let cool.

Once cooled, strain the raspberry mixture through a fine-mesh sieve into a bowl to remove the seeds, pressing down on the solids to extract as much liquid as possible. Discard the seeds and pulp. You should have about 1 cup of raspberry puree. Set aside.

In a separate saucepan, combine the heavy cream, whole milk, granulated sugar, and salt. Heat over medium heat, stirring occasionally, until the mixture begins to steam. Do not let it boil.

Once steaming, remove the saucepan from the heat and stir in the vanilla extract. Let the mixture cool slightly.

Pour the cooled cream mixture into an ice cream maker and churn according to the manufacturer's instructions until it reaches a soft-serve consistency.

Transfer about half of the churned ice cream into a freezer-safe container. Spoon dollops of the raspberry puree over the ice cream. Use a knife or skewer to swirl the raspberry puree into the ice cream.

Add the remaining churned ice cream on top and repeat the process with the remaining raspberry puree, swirling it into the ice cream.

Cover the container with a lid or plastic wrap and freeze for at least 4 hours, or until firm.

Serve and enjoy your homemade Raspberry Swirl Ice Cream!

This recipe yields a creamy vanilla ice cream base with a tart and fruity raspberry swirl running through it, creating a delicious contrast of flavors. It's perfect for enjoying on its own or as a refreshing dessert after a meal. Enjoy!

Blueberry Cheesecake Ice Cream

Ingredients:

For the Blueberry Swirl:

- 2 cups fresh blueberries
- 1/4 cup granulated sugar
- 1 tablespoon lemon juice
- 1 tablespoon water
- 1 teaspoon cornstarch

For the Cheesecake Base:

- 8 ounces cream cheese, softened
- 1 cup heavy cream
- 1 cup whole milk
- 3/4 cup granulated sugar
- Pinch of salt
- 1 teaspoon pure vanilla extract

For the Cheesecake Crust:

- 1 cup graham cracker crumbs
- 2 tablespoons unsalted butter, melted

Instructions:

To make the blueberry swirl, in a saucepan, combine the blueberries, granulated sugar, lemon juice, and water. Cook over medium heat, stirring occasionally, until the blueberries begin to burst and release their juices, about 5 minutes.
In a small bowl, mix the cornstarch with 1 tablespoon of water to create a slurry. Stir the slurry into the blueberry mixture and continue to cook, stirring constantly, until the mixture thickens, about 1-2 minutes. Remove from heat and let cool.
In a mixing bowl, beat the softened cream cheese until smooth and creamy.
In a separate bowl, whisk together the heavy cream, whole milk, granulated sugar, salt, and vanilla extract until the sugar is dissolved.
Gradually add the cream mixture to the beaten cream cheese, whisking until smooth and well combined.

Pour the cheesecake base into an ice cream maker and churn according to the manufacturer's instructions until it reaches a soft-serve consistency.

In a small bowl, mix together the graham cracker crumbs and melted butter until well combined.

Once the ice cream reaches a soft-serve consistency, transfer about half of it to a freezer-safe container. Sprinkle half of the graham cracker mixture over the ice cream and drizzle with half of the cooled blueberry swirl. Repeat the layers with the remaining ice cream, graham cracker mixture, and blueberry swirl.

Use a knife or skewer to gently swirl the blueberry mixture into the ice cream, creating a marbled effect.

Cover the container with a lid or plastic wrap and freeze for at least 4 hours, or until firm.

Serve and enjoy your homemade Blueberry Cheesecake Ice Cream!

This recipe yields a creamy cheesecake-flavored ice cream with swirls of tangy blueberry compote and crunchy graham cracker crumbs, reminiscent of classic blueberry cheesecake. It's a delightful treat that's perfect for any occasion. Enjoy!

Caramel Swirl Ice Cream

Ingredients:

For the Caramel Sauce:

- 1 cup granulated sugar
- 1/4 cup water
- 1/2 cup heavy cream
- 2 tablespoons unsalted butter
- Pinch of salt
- 1 teaspoon vanilla extract

For the Ice Cream Base:

- 2 cups heavy cream
- 1 cup whole milk
- 3/4 cup granulated sugar
- Pinch of salt
- 1 teaspoon pure vanilla extract

Instructions:

Start by making the caramel sauce. In a saucepan, combine the granulated sugar and water over medium heat. Stir until the sugar is dissolved.

Once the sugar is dissolved, stop stirring and let the mixture come to a boil. Allow it to boil, without stirring, until it turns a deep amber color, swirling the pan occasionally to ensure even heating. This may take about 5-7 minutes.

Once the caramel reaches the desired color, remove the saucepan from heat and carefully pour in the heavy cream. Be cautious as the mixture will bubble up.

Stir the mixture until the caramel is fully combined with the cream. If there are any clumps of caramel, return the pan to low heat and stir until they dissolve.

Remove the caramel sauce from heat and stir in the butter, salt, and vanilla extract until smooth. Let the caramel sauce cool to room temperature.

In a separate bowl, whisk together the heavy cream, whole milk, granulated sugar, salt, and vanilla extract until the sugar is dissolved.

Pour the cream mixture into an ice cream maker and churn according to the manufacturer's instructions until it reaches a soft-serve consistency.

Transfer about one-third of the churned ice cream into a freezer-safe container. Drizzle a generous amount of caramel sauce over the ice cream.

Repeat the layers with another one-third of the ice cream and more caramel sauce. Then, add the remaining ice cream on top and drizzle with the remaining caramel sauce.

Use a knife or skewer to gently swirl the caramel into the ice cream, creating a marbled effect.

Cover the container with a lid or plastic wrap and freeze for at least 4 hours, or until firm.

Serve and enjoy your homemade Caramel Swirl Ice Cream!

This recipe yields a creamy vanilla ice cream with ribbons of rich and buttery caramel throughout. It's a decadent treat that's perfect for satisfying your sweet cravings. Enjoy!

Banana Nut Ice Cream

Ingredients:

- 2 ripe bananas, peeled and sliced
- 2 tablespoons lemon juice
- 2 cups heavy cream
- 1 cup whole milk
- 3/4 cup granulated sugar
- Pinch of salt
- 1 teaspoon pure vanilla extract
- 1/2 cup chopped nuts (such as walnuts or pecans)

Instructions:

In a bowl, toss the sliced bananas with lemon juice to prevent browning. Set aside.
In a blender or food processor, puree the bananas until smooth.
In a medium saucepan, combine the heavy cream, whole milk, granulated sugar, and salt. Heat the mixture over medium heat, stirring occasionally, until it begins to steam. Do not let it boil.
Once steaming, remove the saucepan from the heat and stir in the banana puree and vanilla extract. Stir until well combined.
Transfer the mixture to a heatproof bowl and cover with plastic wrap, pressing the plastic wrap directly onto the surface of the mixture to prevent a skin from forming. Chill in the refrigerator for at least 4 hours, or overnight, until thoroughly chilled.
Once chilled, pour the mixture into an ice cream maker and churn according to the manufacturer's instructions until it reaches a soft-serve consistency.
During the last few minutes of churning, add the chopped nuts to the ice cream maker and continue churning until evenly distributed.
Transfer the churned ice cream to a freezer-safe container, cover with a lid or plastic wrap, and freeze for at least 4 hours, or until firm.
Serve and enjoy your homemade Banana Nut Ice Cream!

This recipe yields a creamy banana-flavored ice cream with crunchy bits of chopped nuts throughout. It's a delicious and refreshing treat that's perfect for banana and nut lovers alike. Enjoy!

Lemon Sorbet Ice Cream

Ingredients:

- 1 cup fresh lemon juice (from about 4-6 lemons)
- Zest of 2 lemons
- 1 1/2 cups granulated sugar
- 2 cups water

Instructions:

In a saucepan, combine the water and granulated sugar. Heat over medium heat, stirring occasionally, until the sugar is completely dissolved and the mixture comes to a simmer. Simmer for 2-3 minutes.

Remove the saucepan from the heat and let the sugar syrup cool to room temperature.

Once cooled, stir in the fresh lemon juice and lemon zest until well combined.

Transfer the mixture to a shallow, freezer-safe container and place it in the freezer.

Every 30 minutes, remove the container from the freezer and use a fork to scrape and stir the mixture, breaking up any ice crystals that form. Repeat this process every 30 minutes for about 2-3 hours, or until the sorbet reaches a smooth and creamy consistency.

Once the sorbet is smooth and creamy, transfer it to a freezer-safe container with a lid and freeze for at least 4 hours, or until firm.

Serve and enjoy your homemade Lemon Sorbet Ice Cream!

This recipe yields a tangy and refreshing lemon sorbet ice cream with bright citrus flavor and a smooth texture. It's perfect for hot summer days or as a light and refreshing dessert after a meal. Enjoy!

Orange Creamsicle Ice Cream

Ingredients:

- 2 cups heavy cream
- 1 cup whole milk
- 3/4 cup granulated sugar
- Pinch of salt
- Zest of 2 oranges
- 1/2 cup freshly squeezed orange juice (from about 2-3 oranges)
- 1 teaspoon pure vanilla extract

Instructions:

In a medium saucepan, combine the heavy cream, whole milk, granulated sugar, salt, and orange zest. Heat the mixture over medium heat, stirring occasionally, until it begins to steam. Do not let it boil.

Once steaming, remove the saucepan from the heat and stir in the freshly squeezed orange juice and vanilla extract. Stir until well combined.

Transfer the mixture to a heatproof bowl and cover with plastic wrap, pressing the plastic wrap directly onto the surface of the mixture to prevent a skin from forming. Chill in the refrigerator for at least 4 hours, or overnight, until thoroughly chilled.

Once chilled, pour the mixture into an ice cream maker and churn according to the manufacturer's instructions until it reaches a soft-serve consistency.

Transfer the churned ice cream to a freezer-safe container, cover with a lid or plastic wrap, and freeze for at least 4 hours, or until firm.

Serve and enjoy your homemade Orange Creamsicle Ice Cream!

This recipe yields a creamy and refreshing ice cream with the bright and tangy flavor of fresh oranges and a hint of vanilla reminiscent of the classic creamsicle treat. It's perfect for cooling off on a hot day or as a nostalgic dessert for any occasion. Enjoy!

Almond Joy Ice Cream

Ingredients:

- 2 cups heavy cream
- 1 cup whole milk
- 3/4 cup granulated sugar
- Pinch of salt
- 1 teaspoon pure vanilla extract
- 1/2 cup sweetened shredded coconut
- 1/2 cup chopped almonds
- 1/2 cup chocolate chips (semisweet or milk chocolate)

Instructions:

In a medium saucepan, combine the heavy cream, whole milk, granulated sugar, and salt. Heat the mixture over medium heat, stirring occasionally, until it begins to steam. Do not let it boil.

Once steaming, remove the saucepan from the heat and stir in the vanilla extract. Transfer the mixture to a heatproof bowl and cover with plastic wrap, pressing the plastic wrap directly onto the surface of the mixture to prevent a skin from forming. Chill in the refrigerator for at least 4 hours, or overnight, until thoroughly chilled.

While the ice cream base is chilling, spread the shredded coconut and chopped almonds on a baking sheet. Toast in the oven at 350°F (175°C) for about 5-7 minutes, or until golden brown, stirring occasionally to ensure even toasting. Let them cool completely.

Once the ice cream base is chilled, pour it into an ice cream maker and churn according to the manufacturer's instructions until it reaches a soft-serve consistency.

During the last few minutes of churning, add the toasted shredded coconut, chopped almonds, and chocolate chips to the ice cream maker. Continue churning until evenly distributed.

Transfer the churned ice cream to a freezer-safe container, cover with a lid or plastic wrap, and freeze for at least 4 hours, or until firm.

Serve and enjoy your homemade Almond Joy Ice Cream!

This recipe yields a creamy coconut-flavored ice cream with crunchy almonds and chocolate chips throughout, reminiscent of the beloved Almond Joy candy bar. It's a delightful treat that's perfect for any occasion. Enjoy!

Chocolate Chip Cookie Dough Ice Cream

Ingredients:

For the Cookie Dough:

- 1/2 cup unsalted butter, softened
- 1/2 cup packed light brown sugar
- 1/4 cup granulated sugar
- 1 teaspoon vanilla extract
- 1 cup all-purpose flour
- 1/4 teaspoon salt
- 1/2 cup mini chocolate chips

For the Ice Cream Base:

- 2 cups heavy cream
- 1 cup whole milk
- 3/4 cup granulated sugar
- Pinch of salt
- 2 teaspoons pure vanilla extract

Instructions:

In a mixing bowl, beat the softened butter, brown sugar, and granulated sugar together until light and fluffy. Mix in the vanilla extract.

Gradually add the flour and salt to the butter-sugar mixture, mixing until well combined. Fold in the mini chocolate chips. The dough will be slightly crumbly. If it's too dry, you can add a tablespoon of milk to help bind it together.

Form the cookie dough into small balls, about the size of a teaspoon, and place them on a baking sheet lined with parchment paper. Place the baking sheet in the freezer while you prepare the ice cream base.

In a separate bowl, whisk together the heavy cream, whole milk, granulated sugar, salt, and vanilla extract until the sugar is dissolved.

Pour the cream mixture into an ice cream maker and churn according to the manufacturer's instructions until it reaches a soft-serve consistency.

Once the ice cream reaches the soft-serve stage, remove the cookie dough balls from the freezer. Fold them into the churned ice cream gently, distributing them evenly.

Transfer the ice cream to a freezer-safe container, cover with a lid or plastic wrap, and freeze for at least 4 hours, or until firm.

Serve and enjoy your homemade Chocolate Chip Cookie Dough Ice Cream!

This recipe yields a creamy vanilla ice cream base with chunks of edible cookie dough throughout, making it a delightful treat for any occasion. Enjoy the combination of smooth ice cream and chewy cookie dough pieces!

Key Lime Pie Ice Cream

Ingredients:

For the Ice Cream Base:

- 2 cups heavy cream
- 1 cup whole milk
- 3/4 cup granulated sugar
- Pinch of salt
- Zest of 2 limes
- 1/2 cup fresh lime juice (from about 4-5 key limes or 2-3 regular limes)
- 1 teaspoon pure vanilla extract

For the Graham Cracker Crust:

- 1 1/2 cups graham cracker crumbs
- 1/4 cup granulated sugar
- 6 tablespoons unsalted butter, melted

Instructions:

In a medium saucepan, combine the heavy cream, whole milk, granulated sugar, salt, and lime zest. Heat the mixture over medium heat, stirring occasionally, until it begins to steam. Do not let it boil.

Once steaming, remove the saucepan from the heat and stir in the fresh lime juice and vanilla extract. Stir until well combined.

Transfer the mixture to a heatproof bowl and cover with plastic wrap, pressing the plastic wrap directly onto the surface of the mixture to prevent a skin from forming. Chill in the refrigerator for at least 4 hours, or overnight, until thoroughly chilled.

While the ice cream base is chilling, preheat your oven to 350°F (175°C).

In a mixing bowl, combine the graham cracker crumbs, granulated sugar, and melted butter until well mixed.

Press the graham cracker mixture into the bottom of a 9x9 inch baking dish lined with parchment paper. Bake for 10-12 minutes, or until lightly golden brown. Remove from the oven and let cool completely.

Once the graham cracker crust has cooled, break it into small pieces using a fork or your hands.

Once the ice cream base is thoroughly chilled, pour it into an ice cream maker and churn according to the manufacturer's instructions until it reaches a soft-serve consistency.

During the last few minutes of churning, add the cooled graham cracker crust pieces to the ice cream maker and continue churning until evenly distributed.

Transfer the churned ice cream to a freezer-safe container, cover with a lid or plastic wrap, and freeze for at least 4 hours, or until firm.

Serve and enjoy your homemade Key Lime Pie Ice Cream!

This recipe yields a creamy and tangy lime-flavored ice cream with crunchy bits of graham cracker crust throughout, reminiscent of the classic key lime pie dessert. It's a delightful treat that's perfect for any occasion. Enjoy!

Red Velvet Ice Cream

Ingredients:

For the Ice Cream Base:

- 2 cups heavy cream
- 1 cup whole milk
- 3/4 cup granulated sugar
- Pinch of salt
- 1 teaspoon pure vanilla extract
- 2 tablespoons unsweetened cocoa powder
- 1 tablespoon red food coloring

For the Red Velvet Cake Crumbs:

- 1 cup all-purpose flour
- 3/4 cup granulated sugar
- 1/4 cup unsweetened cocoa powder
- 1/2 teaspoon baking soda
- 1/4 teaspoon salt
- 1/2 cup vegetable oil
- 1/2 cup buttermilk
- 1 large egg
- 1 tablespoon red food coloring
- 1 teaspoon pure vanilla extract
- 1 teaspoon distilled white vinegar

Instructions:

Start by preparing the red velvet cake crumbs. Preheat your oven to 350°F (175°C). Grease and flour an 8x8 inch baking pan.
In a mixing bowl, whisk together the flour, sugar, cocoa powder, baking soda, and salt.
In a separate bowl, whisk together the vegetable oil, buttermilk, egg, red food coloring, vanilla extract, and white vinegar until well combined.
Gradually add the wet ingredients to the dry ingredients, stirring until just combined.

Pour the batter into the prepared baking pan and spread it evenly. Bake in the preheated oven for 20-25 minutes, or until a toothpick inserted into the center comes out clean.

Remove the cake from the oven and let it cool completely. Once cooled, break the cake into small crumbs using a fork or your hands. Set aside.

In a medium saucepan, combine the heavy cream, whole milk, granulated sugar, salt, vanilla extract, cocoa powder, and red food coloring. Heat the mixture over medium heat, stirring occasionally, until it begins to steam. Do not let it boil.

Once steaming, remove the saucepan from the heat and let the mixture cool to room temperature.

Once cooled, pour the mixture into an ice cream maker and churn according to the manufacturer's instructions until it reaches a soft-serve consistency.

During the last few minutes of churning, add the red velvet cake crumbs to the ice cream maker and continue churning until evenly distributed.

Transfer the churned ice cream to a freezer-safe container, cover with a lid or plastic wrap, and freeze for at least 4 hours, or until firm.

Serve and enjoy your homemade Red Velvet Ice Cream!

This recipe yields a creamy and indulgent red velvet-flavored ice cream with the classic taste of red velvet cake crumbs mixed throughout. It's a delightful treat that's perfect for any red velvet lover. Enjoy!

Tiramisu Ice Cream

Ingredients:

For the Ice Cream Base:

- 2 cups heavy cream
- 1 cup whole milk
- 3/4 cup granulated sugar
- Pinch of salt
- 2 teaspoons instant espresso powder (or instant coffee powder)
- 2 tablespoons coffee liqueur (such as Kahlua), optional
- 1 teaspoon pure vanilla extract

For the Tiramisu Swirl:

- 1/2 cup mascarpone cheese
- 1/4 cup powdered sugar
- 2 tablespoons coffee liqueur (such as Kahlua)
- 1/2 cup brewed strong coffee, cooled

For the Tiramisu Layer:

- Ladyfingers (about 10-12), halved horizontally

Instructions:

In a medium saucepan, combine the heavy cream, whole milk, granulated sugar, salt, instant espresso powder, and coffee liqueur (if using). Heat the mixture over medium heat, stirring occasionally, until it begins to steam. Do not let it boil.
Once steaming, remove the saucepan from the heat and stir in the vanilla extract. Let the mixture cool to room temperature.
While the ice cream base is cooling, prepare the tiramisu swirl. In a mixing bowl, whisk together the mascarpone cheese, powdered sugar, and coffee liqueur until smooth and creamy.
Gradually whisk in the brewed coffee until well combined. Set aside.

Once the ice cream base has cooled to room temperature, pour it into an ice cream maker and churn according to the manufacturer's instructions until it reaches a soft-serve consistency.

Once the ice cream reaches the soft-serve stage, transfer about half of it to a freezer-safe container. Spoon dollops of the tiramisu swirl mixture over the ice cream.

Add a layer of halved ladyfingers on top of the swirl mixture.

Repeat the layers with the remaining ice cream and swirl mixture, ending with a final layer of ladyfingers on top.

Cover the container with a lid or plastic wrap and freeze for at least 4 hours, or until firm.

Serve and enjoy your homemade Tiramisu Ice Cream!

This recipe yields a creamy and decadent ice cream with layers of tiramisu swirl and chunks of ladyfingers, capturing the flavors of the classic Italian dessert. It's a delightful treat that's perfect for any occasion. Enjoy!

Sorbet Recipes:

Lemon Sorbet

Ingredients:

- 1 cup granulated sugar
- 1 cup water
- 1 cup freshly squeezed lemon juice (from about 4-6 lemons)
- Zest of 1 lemon

Instructions:

In a small saucepan, combine the granulated sugar and water. Heat over medium heat, stirring occasionally, until the sugar is completely dissolved and the mixture forms a syrup. This usually takes about 3-5 minutes. Remove from heat and let the syrup cool to room temperature.

Once the syrup has cooled, stir in the freshly squeezed lemon juice and lemon zest until well combined.

Transfer the lemon mixture to an ice cream maker and churn according to the manufacturer's instructions until it reaches a sorbet consistency. This typically takes about 20-25 minutes.

Once churned, transfer the lemon sorbet to a freezer-safe container. Cover with a lid or plastic wrap, pressing it directly onto the surface of the sorbet to prevent ice crystals from forming.

Freeze the sorbet for at least 4 hours, or until firm.

Serve the lemon sorbet scoops in chilled bowls and garnish with fresh mint leaves or lemon zest if desired.

This lemon sorbet is wonderfully tangy, refreshing, and perfect for enjoying on a hot day or as a palate cleanser between courses during a meal. Enjoy!

Raspberry Sorbet

Ingredients:

- 3 cups fresh or frozen raspberries
- 1 cup granulated sugar
- 1 cup water
- 2 tablespoons freshly squeezed lemon juice

Instructions:

In a small saucepan, combine the granulated sugar and water. Heat over medium heat, stirring occasionally, until the sugar is completely dissolved and the mixture forms a syrup. This usually takes about 3-5 minutes. Remove from heat and let the syrup cool to room temperature.

In a blender or food processor, puree the raspberries until smooth.

Strain the raspberry puree through a fine-mesh sieve into a large bowl to remove the seeds, pressing down on the solids to extract as much liquid as possible. Discard the seeds.

Stir the cooled sugar syrup and freshly squeezed lemon juice into the raspberry puree until well combined.

Transfer the raspberry mixture to an ice cream maker and churn according to the manufacturer's instructions until it reaches a sorbet consistency. This typically takes about 20-25 minutes.

Once churned, transfer the raspberry sorbet to a freezer-safe container. Cover with a lid or plastic wrap, pressing it directly onto the surface of the sorbet to prevent ice crystals from forming.

Freeze the sorbet for at least 4 hours, or until firm.

Serve the raspberry sorbet scoops in chilled bowls and garnish with fresh raspberries or mint leaves if desired.

This raspberry sorbet is wonderfully refreshing, bursting with fruity flavor, and perfect for enjoying on a hot day or as a light and refreshing dessert after a meal. Enjoy!

Mango Sorbet

Ingredients:

- 4 cups ripe mango chunks (fresh or frozen)
- 1/2 cup granulated sugar (adjust according to the sweetness of your mangoes)
- 1/4 cup water
- 2 tablespoons freshly squeezed lime juice
- Zest of 1 lime (optional)

Instructions:

If using fresh mangoes, peel and chop them into chunks. If using frozen mango chunks, let them thaw slightly.

In a small saucepan, combine the granulated sugar and water. Heat over medium heat, stirring occasionally, until the sugar is completely dissolved and the mixture forms a syrup. This usually takes about 3-5 minutes. Remove from heat and let the syrup cool to room temperature.

In a blender or food processor, puree the mango chunks until smooth.

Strain the mango puree through a fine-mesh sieve into a large bowl to remove any fibers or stringy bits. This step is optional but helps create a smoother sorbet.

Stir the cooled sugar syrup and freshly squeezed lime juice (and lime zest, if using) into the mango puree until well combined.

Taste the mixture and adjust the sweetness or tartness by adding more sugar or lime juice if desired.

Transfer the mango mixture to an ice cream maker and churn according to the manufacturer's instructions until it reaches a sorbet consistency. This typically takes about 20-25 minutes.

Once churned, transfer the mango sorbet to a freezer-safe container. Cover with a lid or plastic wrap, pressing it directly onto the surface of the sorbet to prevent ice crystals from forming.

Freeze the sorbet for at least 4 hours, or until firm.

Serve the mango sorbet scoops in chilled bowls and garnish with fresh mint leaves or additional mango chunks if desired.

This mango sorbet is wonderfully refreshing, bursting with tropical flavor, and perfect for enjoying on a hot day or as a light and refreshing dessert after a meal. Enjoy!

Strawberry Sorbet

Ingredients:

- 1 kg (about 2.2 pounds) fresh strawberries, hulled and halved
- 1 cup granulated sugar
- 1/4 cup freshly squeezed lemon juice
- 1/2 cup water

Instructions:

In a small saucepan, combine the granulated sugar and water. Heat over medium heat, stirring occasionally, until the sugar is completely dissolved. Remove from heat and let the syrup cool to room temperature.

In a blender or food processor, puree the strawberries until smooth.

Strain the strawberry puree through a fine-mesh sieve into a large bowl to remove the seeds, pressing down on the solids to extract as much liquid as possible. Discard the seeds.

Stir the cooled sugar syrup and freshly squeezed lemon juice into the strawberry puree until well combined.

Transfer the strawberry mixture to an ice cream maker and churn according to the manufacturer's instructions until it reaches a sorbet consistency. This typically takes about 20-25 minutes.

Once churned, transfer the strawberry sorbet to a freezer-safe container. Cover with a lid or plastic wrap, pressing it directly onto the surface of the sorbet to prevent ice crystals from forming.

Freeze the sorbet for at least 4 hours, or until firm.

Serve the strawberry sorbet scoops in chilled bowls and garnish with fresh strawberries or mint leaves if desired.

This strawberry sorbet is wonderfully refreshing, bursting with fruity flavor, and perfect for enjoying on a hot day or as a light and refreshing dessert after a meal. Enjoy!

Orange Sorbet

Ingredients:

- 2 cups freshly squeezed orange juice (from about 8-10 oranges)
- 1 cup water
- 1 cup granulated sugar
- Zest of 1 orange
- 2 tablespoons freshly squeezed lemon juice

Instructions:

In a small saucepan, combine the water and granulated sugar. Heat over medium heat, stirring occasionally, until the sugar is completely dissolved. Remove from heat and let the syrup cool to room temperature.

In a large bowl, combine the freshly squeezed orange juice, orange zest, lemon juice, and the cooled sugar syrup. Stir until well combined.

Transfer the orange mixture to an ice cream maker and churn according to the manufacturer's instructions until it reaches a sorbet consistency. This typically takes about 20-25 minutes.

Once churned, transfer the orange sorbet to a freezer-safe container. Cover with a lid or plastic wrap, pressing it directly onto the surface of the sorbet to prevent ice crystals from forming.

Freeze the sorbet for at least 4 hours, or until firm.

Serve the orange sorbet scoops in chilled bowls and garnish with fresh orange slices or mint leaves if desired.

This orange sorbet is wonderfully refreshing, bursting with citrus flavor, and perfect for enjoying on a hot day or as a light and refreshing dessert after a meal. Enjoy!

Watermelon Sorbet

Ingredients:

- 4 cups cubed seedless watermelon (about 1/2 medium-sized watermelon)
- 1/2 cup granulated sugar
- 1/4 cup freshly squeezed lime juice
- Zest of 1 lime
- 1/4 cup water

Instructions:

In a small saucepan, combine the granulated sugar, water, and lime zest. Heat over medium heat, stirring occasionally, until the sugar is completely dissolved. Remove from heat and let the syrup cool to room temperature.

In a blender or food processor, puree the cubed watermelon until smooth.

Strain the watermelon puree through a fine-mesh sieve into a large bowl to remove any pulp or seeds.

Stir the cooled sugar syrup and freshly squeezed lime juice into the watermelon puree until well combined.

Transfer the watermelon mixture to an ice cream maker and churn according to the manufacturer's instructions until it reaches a sorbet consistency. This typically takes about 20-25 minutes.

Once churned, transfer the watermelon sorbet to a freezer-safe container. Cover with a lid or plastic wrap, pressing it directly onto the surface of the sorbet to prevent ice crystals from forming.

Freeze the sorbet for at least 4 hours, or until firm.

Serve the watermelon sorbet scoops in chilled bowls and garnish with fresh mint leaves or lime slices if desired.

This watermelon sorbet is wonderfully refreshing, bursting with fruity flavor, and perfect for enjoying on a hot day or as a light and refreshing dessert after a meal. Enjoy!

Kiwi Sorbet

Ingredients:

- 6 kiwifruits, peeled and chopped
- 1/2 cup granulated sugar
- 1/4 cup water
- 2 tablespoons freshly squeezed lemon juice

Instructions:

In a small saucepan, combine the granulated sugar and water. Heat over medium heat, stirring occasionally, until the sugar is completely dissolved. Remove from heat and let the syrup cool to room temperature.

In a blender or food processor, puree the chopped kiwifruits until smooth.

Strain the kiwi puree through a fine-mesh sieve into a large bowl to remove any seeds or pulp.

Stir the cooled sugar syrup and freshly squeezed lemon juice into the kiwi puree until well combined.

Transfer the kiwi mixture to an ice cream maker and churn according to the manufacturer's instructions until it reaches a sorbet consistency. This typically takes about 20-25 minutes.

Once churned, transfer the kiwi sorbet to a freezer-safe container. Cover with a lid or plastic wrap, pressing it directly onto the surface of the sorbet to prevent ice crystals from forming.

Freeze the sorbet for at least 4 hours, or until firm.

Serve the kiwi sorbet scoops in chilled bowls and garnish with fresh kiwi slices or mint leaves if desired.

This kiwi sorbet is wonderfully refreshing, bursting with tropical flavor, and perfect for enjoying on a hot day or as a light and refreshing dessert after a meal. Enjoy!

Blueberry Sorbet

Ingredients:

- 4 cups fresh or frozen blueberries
- 1 cup granulated sugar
- 1/2 cup water
- 2 tablespoons freshly squeezed lemon juice
- Zest of 1 lemon

Instructions:

In a small saucepan, combine the granulated sugar, water, lemon juice, and lemon zest. Heat over medium heat, stirring occasionally, until the sugar is completely dissolved. Remove from heat and let the syrup cool to room temperature.
In a blender or food processor, puree the blueberries until smooth.
Strain the blueberry puree through a fine-mesh sieve into a large bowl to remove any skins or pulp.
Stir the cooled sugar syrup into the blueberry puree until well combined.
Transfer the blueberry mixture to an ice cream maker and churn according to the manufacturer's instructions until it reaches a sorbet consistency. This typically takes about 20-25 minutes.
Once churned, transfer the blueberry sorbet to a freezer-safe container. Cover with a lid or plastic wrap, pressing it directly onto the surface of the sorbet to prevent ice crystals from forming.
Freeze the sorbet for at least 4 hours, or until firm.
Serve the blueberry sorbet scoops in chilled bowls and garnish with fresh blueberries or lemon zest if desired.

This blueberry sorbet is wonderfully refreshing, bursting with fruity flavor, and perfect for enjoying on a hot day or as a light and refreshing dessert after a meal. Enjoy!

Peach Sorbet

Ingredients:

- 4 cups ripe peaches, peeled, pitted, and chopped (about 5-6 peaches)
- 1 cup granulated sugar
- 1/2 cup water
- 2 tablespoons freshly squeezed lemon juice

Instructions:

In a small saucepan, combine the granulated sugar and water. Heat over medium heat, stirring occasionally, until the sugar is completely dissolved. Remove from heat and let the syrup cool to room temperature.

In a blender or food processor, puree the chopped peaches until smooth.

Strain the peach puree through a fine-mesh sieve into a large bowl to remove any skins or pulp.

Stir the cooled sugar syrup and freshly squeezed lemon juice into the peach puree until well combined.

Transfer the peach mixture to an ice cream maker and churn according to the manufacturer's instructions until it reaches a sorbet consistency. This typically takes about 20-25 minutes.

Once churned, transfer the peach sorbet to a freezer-safe container. Cover with a lid or plastic wrap, pressing it directly onto the surface of the sorbet to prevent ice crystals from forming.

Freeze the sorbet for at least 4 hours, or until firm.

Serve the peach sorbet scoops in chilled bowls and garnish with fresh peach slices or mint leaves if desired.

This peach sorbet is wonderfully refreshing, bursting with fruity flavor, and perfect for enjoying on a hot day or as a light and refreshing dessert after a meal. Enjoy!

Blackberry Sorbet

Ingredients:

- 4 cups fresh blackberries
- 1 cup granulated sugar
- 1/2 cup water
- 2 tablespoons freshly squeezed lemon juice

Instructions:

In a small saucepan, combine the granulated sugar and water. Heat over medium heat, stirring occasionally, until the sugar is completely dissolved. Remove from heat and let the syrup cool to room temperature.

Rinse the blackberries thoroughly under cold water and drain them.

In a blender or food processor, puree the blackberries until smooth.

Strain the blackberry puree through a fine-mesh sieve into a large bowl to remove any seeds or pulp.

Stir the cooled sugar syrup and freshly squeezed lemon juice into the blackberry puree until well combined.

Transfer the blackberry mixture to an ice cream maker and churn according to the manufacturer's instructions until it reaches a sorbet consistency. This typically takes about 20-25 minutes.

Once churned, transfer the blackberry sorbet to a freezer-safe container. Cover with a lid or plastic wrap, pressing it directly onto the surface of the sorbet to prevent ice crystals from forming.

Freeze the sorbet for at least 4 hours, or until firm.

Serve the blackberry sorbet scoops in chilled bowls and garnish with fresh blackberries or mint leaves if desired.

This blackberry sorbet is wonderfully refreshing, bursting with fruity flavor, and perfect for enjoying on a hot day or as a light and refreshing dessert after a meal. Enjoy!

Green Apple Sorbet

Ingredients:

- 4 large green apples, peeled, cored, and chopped
- 1 cup granulated sugar
- 1 cup water
- 2 tablespoons freshly squeezed lemon juice
- Zest of 1 lemon (optional, for added flavor)

Instructions:

In a small saucepan, combine the granulated sugar and water. Heat over medium heat, stirring occasionally, until the sugar is completely dissolved. Remove from heat and let the syrup cool to room temperature.

In a blender or food processor, puree the chopped green apples until smooth.

Strain the apple puree through a fine-mesh sieve into a large bowl to remove any pulp or fibers.

Stir the cooled sugar syrup, freshly squeezed lemon juice, and lemon zest (if using) into the apple puree until well combined.

Transfer the apple mixture to an ice cream maker and churn according to the manufacturer's instructions until it reaches a sorbet consistency. This typically takes about 20-25 minutes.

Once churned, transfer the green apple sorbet to a freezer-safe container. Cover with a lid or plastic wrap, pressing it directly onto the surface of the sorbet to prevent ice crystals from forming.

Freeze the sorbet for at least 4 hours, or until firm.

Serve the green apple sorbet scoops in chilled bowls and garnish with fresh apple slices or mint leaves if desired.

This green apple sorbet is wonderfully refreshing, bursting with fruity flavor, and perfect for enjoying on a hot day or as a light and refreshing dessert after a meal. Enjoy!

Grape Sorbet

Ingredients:

- 4 cups seedless grapes (red, green, or a combination), washed and stemmed
- 1 cup granulated sugar
- 1 cup water
- 2 tablespoons freshly squeezed lemon juice

Instructions:

In a small saucepan, combine the granulated sugar and water. Heat over medium heat, stirring occasionally, until the sugar is completely dissolved. Remove from heat and let the syrup cool to room temperature.

In a blender or food processor, puree the grapes until smooth.

Strain the grape puree through a fine-mesh sieve into a large bowl to remove any seeds or pulp.

Stir the cooled sugar syrup and freshly squeezed lemon juice into the grape puree until well combined.

Transfer the grape mixture to an ice cream maker and churn according to the manufacturer's instructions until it reaches a sorbet consistency. This typically takes about 20-25 minutes.

Once churned, transfer the grape sorbet to a freezer-safe container. Cover with a lid or plastic wrap, pressing it directly onto the surface of the sorbet to prevent ice crystals from forming.

Freeze the sorbet for at least 4 hours, or until firm.

Serve the grape sorbet scoops in chilled bowls and garnish with fresh grapes or mint leaves if desired.

This grape sorbet is wonderfully refreshing, bursting with fruity flavor, and perfect for enjoying on a hot day or as a light and refreshing dessert after a meal. Enjoy!

Passion Fruit Sorbet

Ingredients:

- 1 cup passion fruit pulp (about 8-10 passion fruits)
- 1 cup water
- 1 cup granulated sugar
- 2 tablespoons freshly squeezed lime juice

Instructions:

Cut the passion fruits in half and scoop out the pulp into a bowl.

In a small saucepan, combine the water and granulated sugar. Heat over medium heat, stirring occasionally, until the sugar is completely dissolved. Remove from heat and let the syrup cool to room temperature.

Strain the passion fruit pulp through a fine-mesh sieve into a large bowl to remove any seeds.

Stir the cooled sugar syrup and freshly squeezed lime juice into the passion fruit pulp until well combined.

Transfer the passion fruit mixture to an ice cream maker and churn according to the manufacturer's instructions until it reaches a sorbet consistency. This typically takes about 20-25 minutes.

Once churned, transfer the passion fruit sorbet to a freezer-safe container. Cover with a lid or plastic wrap, pressing it directly onto the surface of the sorbet to prevent ice crystals from forming.

Freeze the sorbet for at least 4 hours, or until firm.

Serve the passion fruit sorbet scoops in chilled bowls and garnish with fresh passion fruit seeds or mint leaves if desired.

This passion fruit sorbet is wonderfully refreshing, bursting with tropical flavor, and perfect for enjoying on a hot day or as a light and refreshing dessert after a meal. Enjoy!

Lychee Sorbet

Ingredients:

- 2 cups lychee fruit, peeled, pitted, and roughly chopped (fresh or canned in syrup)
- 1 cup water
- 1/2 cup granulated sugar
- 2 tablespoons freshly squeezed lime juice

Instructions:

In a blender or food processor, puree the lychee fruit until smooth.

In a small saucepan, combine the water and granulated sugar. Heat over medium heat, stirring occasionally, until the sugar is completely dissolved. Remove from heat and let the syrup cool to room temperature.

Strain the lychee puree through a fine-mesh sieve into a large bowl to remove any fibrous bits.

Stir the cooled sugar syrup and freshly squeezed lime juice into the lychee puree until well combined.

Transfer the lychee mixture to an ice cream maker and churn according to the manufacturer's instructions until it reaches a sorbet consistency. This typically takes about 20-25 minutes.

Once churned, transfer the lychee sorbet to a freezer-safe container. Cover with a lid or plastic wrap, pressing it directly onto the surface of the sorbet to prevent ice crystals from forming.

Freeze the sorbet for at least 4 hours, or until firm.

Serve the lychee sorbet scoops in chilled bowls and garnish with fresh lychee fruit or mint leaves if desired.

This lychee sorbet is wonderfully refreshing, with a delicate and exotic flavor that's perfect for enjoying on a hot day or as a light and refreshing dessert after a meal. Enjoy!

Pear Sorbet

Ingredients:

- 4 ripe pears, peeled, cored, and diced
- 1/2 cup granulated sugar
- 1/2 cup water
- 2 tablespoons freshly squeezed lemon juice

Instructions:

In a small saucepan, combine the granulated sugar and water. Heat over medium heat, stirring occasionally, until the sugar is completely dissolved. Remove from heat and let the syrup cool to room temperature.

In a blender or food processor, puree the diced pears until smooth.

Strain the pear puree through a fine-mesh sieve into a large bowl to remove any fibrous bits.

Stir the cooled sugar syrup and freshly squeezed lemon juice into the pear puree until well combined.

Transfer the pear mixture to an ice cream maker and churn according to the manufacturer's instructions until it reaches a sorbet consistency. This typically takes about 20-25 minutes.

Once churned, transfer the pear sorbet to a freezer-safe container. Cover with a lid or plastic wrap, pressing it directly onto the surface of the sorbet to prevent ice crystals from forming.

Freeze the sorbet for at least 4 hours, or until firm.

Serve the pear sorbet scoops in chilled bowls and garnish with fresh pear slices or mint leaves if desired.

This pear sorbet is wonderfully refreshing, with a delicate and fruity flavor that's perfect for enjoying on a hot day or as a light and refreshing dessert after a meal. Enjoy!

Cranberry Sorbet

Ingredients:

- 3 cups fresh or frozen cranberries
- 1 cup water
- 1 cup granulated sugar
- Zest and juice of 1 orange

Instructions:

In a medium saucepan, combine the cranberries, water, sugar, orange zest, and orange juice. Bring the mixture to a boil over medium heat, then reduce the heat to low and simmer for about 10 minutes, or until the cranberries have burst and the mixture has thickened slightly.

Remove the saucepan from the heat and let the cranberry mixture cool to room temperature.

Once cooled, transfer the cranberry mixture to a blender or food processor and blend until smooth.

Strain the cranberry puree through a fine-mesh sieve into a large bowl to remove any skins or pulp.

Transfer the strained cranberry mixture to an ice cream maker and churn according to the manufacturer's instructions until it reaches a sorbet consistency. This typically takes about 20-25 minutes.

Once churned, transfer the cranberry sorbet to a freezer-safe container. Cover with a lid or plastic wrap, pressing it directly onto the surface of the sorbet to prevent ice crystals from forming.

Freeze the sorbet for at least 4 hours, or until firm.

Serve the cranberry sorbet scoops in chilled bowls and garnish with fresh cranberries or orange zest if desired.

This cranberry sorbet is wonderfully refreshing, with a tangy and fruity flavor that's perfect for enjoying on a hot day or as a light and refreshing dessert after a meal. Enjoy!

Pomegranate Sorbet

Ingredients:

- 2 cups pomegranate juice (freshly squeezed or store-bought)
- 1/2 cup water
- 1/2 cup granulated sugar
- Zest and juice of 1 lime or lemon (optional, for added flavor)

Instructions:

In a small saucepan, combine the water and granulated sugar. Heat over medium heat, stirring occasionally, until the sugar is completely dissolved. Remove from heat and let the syrup cool to room temperature.

In a large bowl, mix together the pomegranate juice, cooled sugar syrup, and the zest and juice of one lime or lemon if using. Stir until well combined.

Transfer the mixture to an ice cream maker and churn according to the manufacturer's instructions until it reaches a sorbet consistency. This typically takes about 20-25 minutes.

Once churned, transfer the sorbet to a freezer-safe container. Cover with a lid or plastic wrap, pressing it directly onto the surface of the sorbet to prevent ice crystals from forming.

Freeze the sorbet for at least 4 hours, or until firm.

Serve the pomegranate sorbet scoops in chilled bowls and garnish with fresh pomegranate seeds or a twist of lime or lemon zest if desired.

This pomegranate sorbet is wonderfully refreshing, with a vibrant and tangy flavor that's perfect for enjoying on a hot day or as a light and refreshing dessert after a meal. Enjoy!

Guava Sorbet

Ingredients:

- 4 cups ripe guava pulp (about 8-10 guavas), seeds removed
- 1 cup water
- 1 cup granulated sugar
- 2 tablespoons freshly squeezed lime juice

Instructions:

In a blender or food processor, puree the ripe guava pulp until smooth.
In a small saucepan, combine the water and granulated sugar. Heat over medium heat, stirring occasionally, until the sugar is completely dissolved. Remove from heat and let the syrup cool to room temperature.
Strain the guava puree through a fine-mesh sieve into a large bowl to remove any seeds or fibrous bits.
Stir the cooled sugar syrup and freshly squeezed lime juice into the guava puree until well combined.
Transfer the guava mixture to an ice cream maker and churn according to the manufacturer's instructions until it reaches a sorbet consistency. This typically takes about 20-25 minutes.
Once churned, transfer the guava sorbet to a freezer-safe container. Cover with a lid or plastic wrap, pressing it directly onto the surface of the sorbet to prevent ice crystals from forming.
Freeze the sorbet for at least 4 hours, or until firm.
Serve the guava sorbet scoops in chilled bowls and garnish with fresh guava slices or mint leaves if desired.

This guava sorbet is wonderfully refreshing, with a tropical and fruity flavor that's perfect for enjoying on a hot day or as a light and refreshing dessert after a meal. Enjoy!

Plum Sorbet

Ingredients:

- 4 cups ripe plums, pitted and chopped
- 1 cup water
- 1 cup granulated sugar
- 2 tablespoons freshly squeezed lemon juice

Instructions:

In a small saucepan, combine the water and granulated sugar. Heat over medium heat, stirring occasionally, until the sugar is completely dissolved. Remove from heat and let the syrup cool to room temperature.

In a blender or food processor, puree the chopped plums until smooth.

Strain the plum puree through a fine-mesh sieve into a large bowl to remove any skins or pulp.

Stir the cooled sugar syrup and freshly squeezed lemon juice into the plum puree until well combined.

Transfer the plum mixture to an ice cream maker and churn according to the manufacturer's instructions until it reaches a sorbet consistency. This typically takes about 20-25 minutes.

Once churned, transfer the plum sorbet to a freezer-safe container. Cover with a lid or plastic wrap, pressing it directly onto the surface of the sorbet to prevent ice crystals from forming.

Freeze the sorbet for at least 4 hours, or until firm.

Serve the plum sorbet scoops in chilled bowls and garnish with fresh plum slices or mint leaves if desired.

This plum sorbet is wonderfully refreshing, with a sweet and tangy flavor that's perfect for enjoying on a hot day or as a light and refreshing dessert after a meal. Enjoy!

Cantaloupe Sorbet

Ingredients:

- 1 ripe cantaloupe, peeled, seeded, and cubed (about 4-5 cups)
- 1/2 cup granulated sugar
- 1/2 cup water
- 2 tablespoons freshly squeezed lemon juice

Instructions:

In a small saucepan, combine the granulated sugar and water. Heat over medium heat, stirring occasionally, until the sugar is completely dissolved. Remove from heat and let the syrup cool to room temperature.

In a blender or food processor, puree the cubed cantaloupe until smooth.

Strain the cantaloupe puree through a fine-mesh sieve into a large bowl to remove any fibers.

Stir the cooled sugar syrup and freshly squeezed lemon juice into the cantaloupe puree until well combined.

Transfer the cantaloupe mixture to an ice cream maker and churn according to the manufacturer's instructions until it reaches a sorbet consistency. This typically takes about 20-25 minutes.

Once churned, transfer the cantaloupe sorbet to a freezer-safe container. Cover with a lid or plastic wrap, pressing it directly onto the surface of the sorbet to prevent ice crystals from forming.

Freeze the sorbet for at least 4 hours, or until firm.

Serve the cantaloupe sorbet scoops in chilled bowls and garnish with fresh cantaloupe slices or mint leaves if desired.

This cantaloupe sorbet is wonderfully refreshing, with a sweet and fruity flavor that's perfect for enjoying on a hot day or as a light and refreshing dessert after a meal. Enjoy!

Fig Sorbet

Ingredients:

- 2 cups fresh figs, stemmed and chopped (about 10-12 figs)
- 1 cup water
- 1/2 cup granulated sugar
- 2 tablespoons freshly squeezed lemon juice

Instructions:

In a small saucepan, combine the water and granulated sugar. Heat over medium heat, stirring occasionally, until the sugar is completely dissolved. Remove from heat and let the syrup cool to room temperature.
In a blender or food processor, puree the chopped figs until smooth.
Strain the fig puree through a fine-mesh sieve into a large bowl to remove any seeds or skins.
Stir the cooled sugar syrup and freshly squeezed lemon juice into the fig puree until well combined.
Transfer the fig mixture to an ice cream maker and churn according to the manufacturer's instructions until it reaches a sorbet consistency. This typically takes about 20-25 minutes.
Once churned, transfer the fig sorbet to a freezer-safe container. Cover with a lid or plastic wrap, pressing it directly onto the surface of the sorbet to prevent ice crystals from forming.
Freeze the sorbet for at least 4 hours, or until firm.
Serve the fig sorbet scoops in chilled bowls and garnish with fresh fig slices or mint leaves if desired.

This fig sorbet is wonderfully refreshing, with a unique and delicate flavor that's perfect for enjoying on a hot day or as a light and refreshing dessert after a meal. Enjoy!

Papaya Sorbet

Ingredients:

- 4 cups ripe papaya, peeled, seeded, and chopped
- 1/2 cup granulated sugar
- 1/2 cup water
- 2 tablespoons freshly squeezed lime juice

Instructions:

In a small saucepan, combine the water and granulated sugar. Heat over medium heat, stirring occasionally, until the sugar is completely dissolved. Remove from heat and let the syrup cool to room temperature.

In a blender or food processor, puree the chopped papaya until smooth.

Strain the papaya puree through a fine-mesh sieve into a large bowl to remove any fibrous bits.

Stir the cooled sugar syrup and freshly squeezed lime juice into the papaya puree until well combined.

Transfer the papaya mixture to an ice cream maker and churn according to the manufacturer's instructions until it reaches a sorbet consistency. This typically takes about 20-25 minutes.

Once churned, transfer the papaya sorbet to a freezer-safe container. Cover with a lid or plastic wrap, pressing it directly onto the surface of the sorbet to prevent ice crystals from forming.

Freeze the sorbet for at least 4 hours, or until firm.

Serve the papaya sorbet scoops in chilled bowls and garnish with fresh papaya slices or mint leaves if desired.

This papaya sorbet is wonderfully refreshing, with a tropical and fruity flavor that's perfect for enjoying on a hot day or as a light and refreshing dessert after a meal. Enjoy!

Honeydew Sorbet

Ingredients:

- 1 ripe honeydew melon, peeled, seeded, and chopped (about 4-5 cups)
- 1/2 cup granulated sugar
- 1/2 cup water
- 2 tablespoons freshly squeezed lime juice

Instructions:

In a small saucepan, combine the water and granulated sugar. Heat over medium heat, stirring occasionally, until the sugar is completely dissolved. Remove from heat and let the syrup cool to room temperature.

In a blender or food processor, puree the chopped honeydew melon until smooth. Strain the honeydew puree through a fine-mesh sieve into a large bowl to remove any fibers.

Stir the cooled sugar syrup and freshly squeezed lime juice into the honeydew puree until well combined.

Transfer the honeydew mixture to an ice cream maker and churn according to the manufacturer's instructions until it reaches a sorbet consistency. This typically takes about 20-25 minutes.

Once churned, transfer the honeydew sorbet to a freezer-safe container. Cover with a lid or plastic wrap, pressing it directly onto the surface of the sorbet to prevent ice crystals from forming.

Freeze the sorbet for at least 4 hours, or until firm.

Serve the honeydew sorbet scoops in chilled bowls and garnish with fresh honeydew melon balls or mint leaves if desired.

This honeydew sorbet is wonderfully refreshing, with a sweet and subtle flavor that's perfect for enjoying on a hot day or as a light and refreshing dessert after a meal. Enjoy!

www.ingramcontent.com/pod-product-compliance
Lightning Source LLC
LaVergne TN
LVHW081318060526
838201LV00055B/2345